USBORNE
THE GREAT
WORLD
SEARCH

Kamini Khanduri

Illustrated by David Hancock

Series editor: Felicity Brooks

Contents

About this book

Great Aunt Marigold has given you a wonderful present: a ticket to go on a trip around the world. You will visit lots of exciting places and there are all kinds of things to find and puzzles to solve along the way.

This is Great Aunt Marigold. She'll be coming with you on the trip.

This map of the world shows the places you will stop at on your tour.

Great Aunt Marigold says that in each place, you have to pick up a present for a friend or relation. But she hasn't told you which present is in which place – that's one of the puzzles for you to solve. Here's what you have to find:

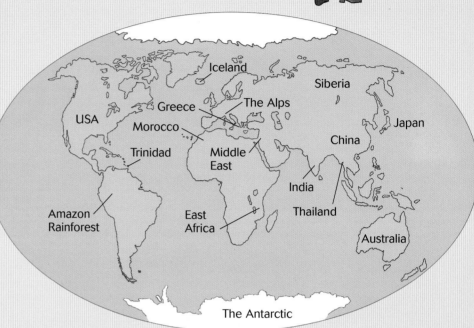

Iceland
Siberia
Greece
The Alps
USA
Morocco
Japan
China
Trinidad
Middle East
India
Thailand
Amazon Rainforest
East Africa
Australia
The Antarctic

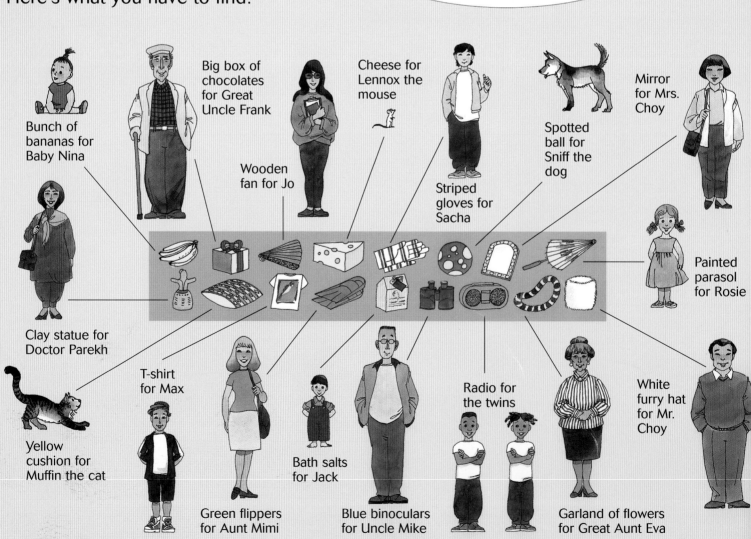

Bunch of bananas for Baby Nina

Big box of chocolates for Great Uncle Frank

Wooden fan for Jo

Cheese for Lennox the mouse

Striped gloves for Sacha

Spotted ball for Sniff the dog

Mirror for Mrs. Choy

Clay statue for Doctor Parekh

Painted parasol for Rosie

Yellow cushion for Muffin the cat

T-shirt for Max

Bath salts for Jack

Radio for the twins

White furry hat for Mr. Choy

Green flippers for Aunt Mimi

Blue binoculars for Uncle Mike

Garland of flowers for Great Aunt Eva

What to spot

Each of the double pages in this book shows a different place on your tour. In each place, there are lots of things to look for. Some things are easy to spot, but some are very tricky. This is how the puzzles work.

This strip tells you where you are, what time it is, and what the weather's like.

This tells you what Great Aunt Marigold is doing. You'll find her in every place.

These little pictures show the things you can find in the big picture.

This box is a reminder of the presents you have to find. There's one present in each place.

The writing next to each little picture tells you how many of that thing to look for in the big picture.

Even if you can only see part of a thing, it still counts.

This tells you to find something you'll need in the next place.

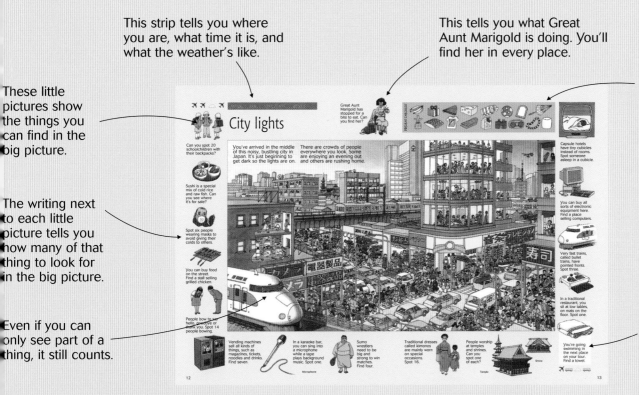

Finding the way

When you've done all the puzzles on a double page, you have to find out where to go next – it won't be the place on the next page in the book. You also need to find how to travel there. Here's what you do.

In the bottom right-hand corner of each double page, four tiny pictures tell you how to travel to the next place.

To find out where to go next, look for exactly the same four pictures in the top left-hand corner of another double page.

You'll travel by train, plane, boat or bus, but you won't use them all on each journey, and you may use any of them more than once.

PUZZLE CHECKLIST

In each place, you must find:
~ Great Aunt Marigold
~ One present for a friend or relation
~ Lots of things hidden in the big picture
~ One thing you'll need in the next place
~ Which place to go to next

If you get stuck finding your way, there's a map showing the correct route on page 40. If you get stuck doing any of the other puzzles, you'll find all the answers on pages 42–47. Now turn the page and begin your journey...

At the airport

Great Aunt Marigold has lots of bags. Find her.

Information about flights is displayed on screens. Can you spot 11?

You can shop for all kinds of things. Find someone buying sunglasses.

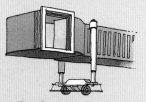

To get onto the plane, you go along a covered walkway. Can you see where it is?

Restaurants serve food and drink. Can you spot someone eating this meal?

Old or disabled people can be driven around in buggies. Spot two.

Some kinds of pets can be taken on planes, but only in special containers. Find this cat.

You're setting off on your exciting trip from a big, busy airport. Outside, the plane is filling up with people. Before getting on board, you must check in your bags and go through security. Then you'll be off!

Bag being searched

Knife showing up on X-ray machine

Security officers check that no one has any weapons. Find these things.

Person going through metal detector

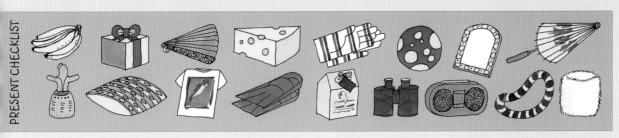

PRESENT CHECKLIST

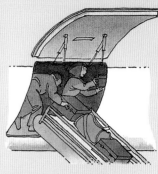

Bags that have been checked in are loaded into the cargo hold of the plane. Find it.

You need a ticket to go on a plane journey. Spot someone who has torn his ticket.

You can wheel your bags around on a trolley. Can you spot seven?

At the bureau de change, you can buy money to use in other countries. Can you find it?

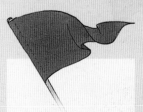

In the first place on your tour, there will be a festival. Find a red flag to wave.

Spot eight telephones.

Flight attendants look after the passengers on planes. Find ten.

Officers in the control tower give instructions to the pilots of the planes. Can you see it?

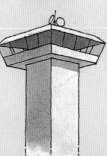

Great Aunt Marigold is dropping her shopping. Find her.

Floating market

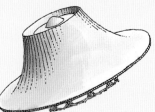

A straw hat will protect you from the sun. Spot two boats selling hats.

Most fruit and vegetables are sold by weight. Spot nine sets of weighing scales.

Can you find 11 purple-throated sunbirds?

You can buy curry with noodles or rice. Find two boats where food is being cooked and sold.

You've taken a trip along a canal to visit this unusual market. Most things here are being sold from boats. If you want to buy something, just call out to the person in the boat. She'll paddle over and you can do your shopping.

Can you spot someone who is selling grilled corn on the cob?

Watermelons

Pineapples

Lots of fresh fruit and vegetables are for sale. Find two boats full of each of these.

Coconuts

Limes

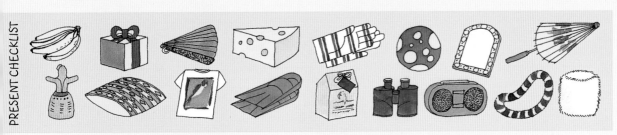

Dolls dressed as traditional Thai dancers are for sale. Can you see where?

Flowers

Pots and pans

Fish

Find three boats selling each of these things in the market.

Buddhist temple

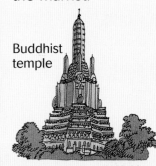

Buddhism is the main religion here, so there are lots of Buddhist temples. Spot one.

In the next place, you'll be going out for the evening. Find this silk jacket to wear.

You can buy all kinds of beautiful handmade crafts. Can you spot these things?

Carved wooden tables

Silver necklaces

Embroidered cushions

Lacquerware ducks

Buddhist monks come out of their temples to ask for food. Spot six.

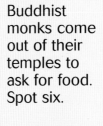

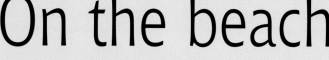
On the beach

Windsurfers sail along, standing on a sailboard. Find ten.

Sunblock

Sunblock protects your skin from the sun. Spot four people putting it on.

Dolphins are very friendly and often swim near people. Spot ten.

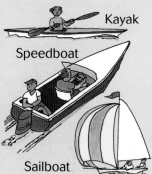

Kayak

Speedboat

Sailboat

There are all kinds of boats here. Find seven of each of these.

Spot 14 seagulls.

It's a hot, sunny summer's day and you've arrived at a very crowded beach. You could go for a swim, or join all the people doing exciting sports in the water. If you're feeling lazy, you could just lie on the sand and relax.

Water-skiers are pulled along the surface of the water by a speedboat. Spot eight.

Teams of lifesavers look out for people in danger. Spot a team doing a practice rescue.

You can go diving around coral reefs to look at the amazing underwater wildlife. Spot five divers.

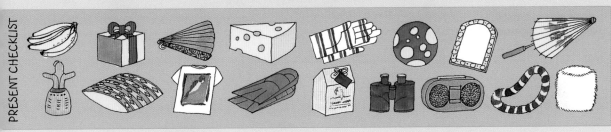

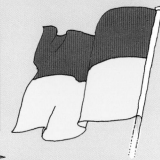

Flags mark out which areas are safe from sharks or dangerous tides. Spot two.

Koala

Kangaroo

Kangaroos and koalas live in the wild in Australia. Can you find a toy one of each?

Surfers skim over the waves on a surfboard. Find 30.

People drive jet skis across the water. Spot nine.

In the next place, there are some unusual birds. Find a camera to take pictures of them.

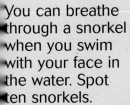

You can breathe through a snorkel when you swim with your face in the water. Spot ten snorkels.

Snorkel

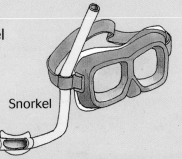

Parasailers have parachutes. A boat pulls them along on the water and they rise into the air. Spot two.

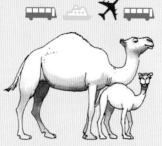

Great Aunt Marigold is being helpful. Can you see where she is?

Desert homes

You've journeyed across the dry, dusty desert to visit the Bedouin people. They usually live in small groups, but today they've come together to prepare for a big festival. The tents are buzzing with all kinds of activity.

The Bedouin take good care of their camels and often give them names. Can you spot 40?

Bedouin foods include meat, rice, cheese and bread. Find someone baking bread.

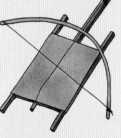

These musical instruments, called rababs, are often played to entertain guests. Find four.

Goats are kept for meat, and their thick hair is woven to make tents. Spot 30.

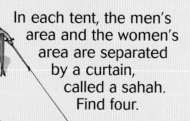

Sahah

In each tent, the men's area and the women's area are separated by a curtain, called a sahah. Find four.

Sacks of dried food

Strings of onions

The Bedouin sell animals and buy some things at markets in towns. Find three of each of these things.

Metal cooking pots

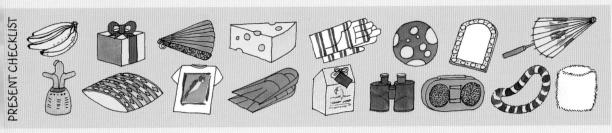

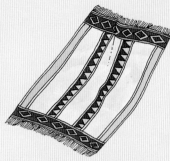

Women weave rugs, saddlebags, cushions and cloth from goat or camel hair. Find this rug.

Today, most Bedouin travel in trucks instead of on camels. Can you find nine?

Fast dogs, called salukis, hunt hares for their owners. Spot ten.

People drink frothy camel milk and also use it for cooking. Spot three bowls of it.

In the next place, you can visit temples. Spot a book telling you where they are.

The Bedouin make coffee for anyone who visits their tent. Find these things.

Coffee pot

Ladle for roasting coffee

Pestle and mortar for grinding coffee

Coffee cups

Can you find three camel saddles?

Great Aunt Marigold has stopped for a bite to eat. Can you find her?

City lights

You've arrived in the middle of this noisy, bustling city in Japan. It's just beginning to get dark so the lights are on.

There are crowds of people everywhere you look. Some are enjoying an evening out and others are rushing home.

Can you spot 20 schoolchildren with their backpacks?

Sushi is a special dish of cold rice and raw fish. Can you see where it is for sale?

Spot six people wearing masks to avoid giving their colds to others.

You can buy food on the street. Find a stall selling grilled chicken.

People bow to say hello, goodbye or thank you. Spot 14 people bowing.

Vending machines sell all kinds of things, such as magazines, tickets, noodles and drinks. Find seven.

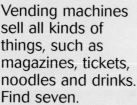

In a karaoke bar, you can sing into a microphone while a tape plays background music. Spot one.

Microphone

Sumo wrestlers need to be big and strong to win matches. Find four.

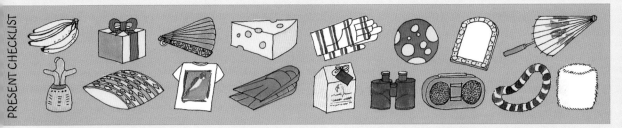

Capsule hotels have tiny cubicles instead of rooms. Spot someone asleep in a cubicle.

You can buy all sorts of electronic equipment here. Find a place selling computers.

Very fast trains, called bullet trains, have pointed fronts. Spot three.

In a traditional restaurant, you need to sit at low tables, on mats on the floor. Spot one.

You're going swimming in the next place on your tour. Find a towel.

Traditional dresses called kimonos are mainly worn on special occasions. Spot 16.

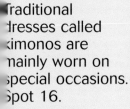

People worship at temples and shrines. Can you spot one of each?

Shrine

Temple

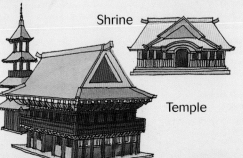

At the pool

Great Aunt Marigold is trying to read. Can you see where she is?

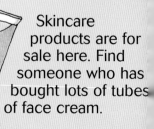

All kinds of birds make their nests on nearby coasts. Spot 20 eider ducks.

Toy shark

Inflatable bed

Many people just come to relax and have fun in the water. Find seven of each of these.

Buoys show you where the water's too hot to swim in, and where it's very shallow. Spot 20.

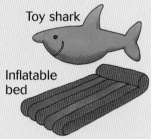

A power station next to the pool uses steam from the hot water. Can you find five pipes blowing out steam?

Horse riding

You can have fun splashing around in this pool called the Blue Lagoon. The hot, salty water comes up from under the ground. Nearby, there are bubbling mud pools and springs that spout steam and boiling water into the air.

There are lots of activities to do in the area. Spot seven people doing each of these things.

Hiking

At the Blue Lagoon Clinic, doctors treat people who have skin problems. Can you see a doctor?

Skincare products are for sale here. Find someone who has bought lots of tubes of face cream.

14

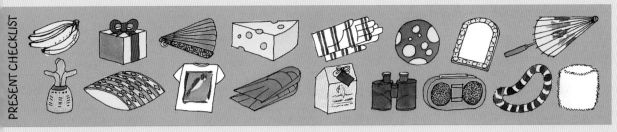

Trucks are good for driving on Iceland's bumpy roads. Spot eight.

These food trays contain Icelandic fish, such as shark, shrimp or salmon. Spot 21.

There are changing rooms where you can leave your clothes. Find the women's one.

You can stay at the Blue Lagoon Hotel. Spot a man who's just arrived with lots of bags.

Next, you're going on a boat. Find some sea-sickness pills in case you feel ill.

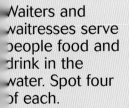

Waiters and waitresses serve people food and drink in the water. Spot four of each.

Both the water and the mud at the bottom of the pool are supposed to be good for your skin. Spot 15 people with mud on their faces.

Great Aunt Marigold is wrapped up warmly. Can you see her?

Frozen land

Albatrosses glide over the water looking for food. Find three.

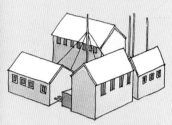

No one lives here all the time, but scientists stay at the research station. Find it.

Killer whales sometimes hunt seals by tipping them off pieces of ice. Spot four.

Castle

Pyramid

Greek temple

Icebergs are huge lumps of ice that float in the sea. Can you find these shapes?

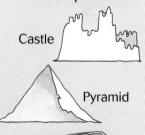

You've come to the cold, windy Antarctic, where the land and sea are nearly always frozen. You can watch whales and take photos of penguins, but you mustn't disturb the animals or spoil their icy home.

"Porpoising" out of the water

Penguins can't fly, but they have other ways of moving fast. Find 12 penguins doing each of these things.

"Tobogganing" across the ice

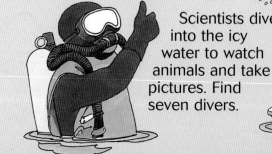

Scientists dive into the icy water to watch animals and take pictures. Find seven divers.

Crabeater seal. Spot 12

16

Scientists go in small planes to do research in very remote areas. Find three.

Find one humpback whale.

Small boats called dinghies are good for finding a way through the icy sea. Spot eight.

Leopard seals are fierce. They often hunt penguins. Can you spot two?

Next, you'll be going to a shady place. Find a flashlight to help you see.

esearch ships carry cientists and their upplies. Cruise ships arry tourists. Spot ne of each.

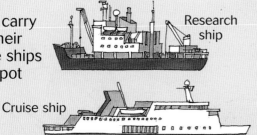

Research ship

Cruise ship

Scientists attach satellite tags to some large animals, to record information about how they live. Spot two.

Carnival!

You've arrived just in time for the Carnival. Hundreds of people are parading along the street in big groups. You can have fun just watching them go by, but the music is so lively, you're bound to start dancing.

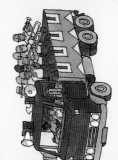

Many costumes cost a lot and take months to make. Spot this amazing one.

The police make sure there is no trouble. Spot ten police officers.

Some musicians travel on trucks called floats. Spot three.

PRESENT CHECKLIST

Great Aunt Marigold is dancing in the crowd. Can you see her?

Underwater

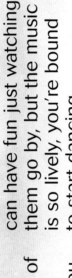

The circus

Incas

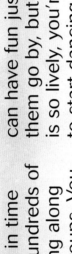

Flying animals

Spanish dancing

Each group has a theme, and the members' costumes show what it is. Find the groups with these themes.

These metal drums are called pans. Spot 18.

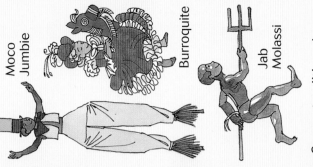

Moco Jumbie

Burroquite

Jab Molassi

Some traditional characters are here every year. Find these.

Next, you'll be doing lots of shopping. Find a calculator to add up what you spend.

Tasty tropical fruits, such as mangoes and pineapples, grow in Trinidad. Find a fruit stall.

Carnival songs, called calypsos, have a strong beat and are good to dance to. Spot two people singing into microphones.

Corn on the cob

Bread called roti

Can you see where people are selling these snacks on the street?

fruit sorbet

Judges decide which group has the best music and costumes. Spot someone pretending to be a judge.

The coconut seller slices the top off coconuts, so you can drink the juice and scoop out the soft, white flesh. Find her.

Shady souk

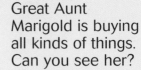 Great Aunt Marigold is buying all kinds of things. Can you see her?

Herbs and spices, such as mint and saffron, look and smell wonderful. Find where they are being sold.

Lute

Drum

You can often hear music in the souk. Find these instruments.

Wool for making carpets is dyed and hung up to dry. Spot three people carrying bundles of wool.

Dates grow in the desert, on date palm trees. Can you see some dates for sale?

You've arrived in the middle of a busy Moroccan market, called a souk. There are lots of unusual things for sale. You can wander slowly down the shady passageways and take in all the interesting sights, smells and noises.

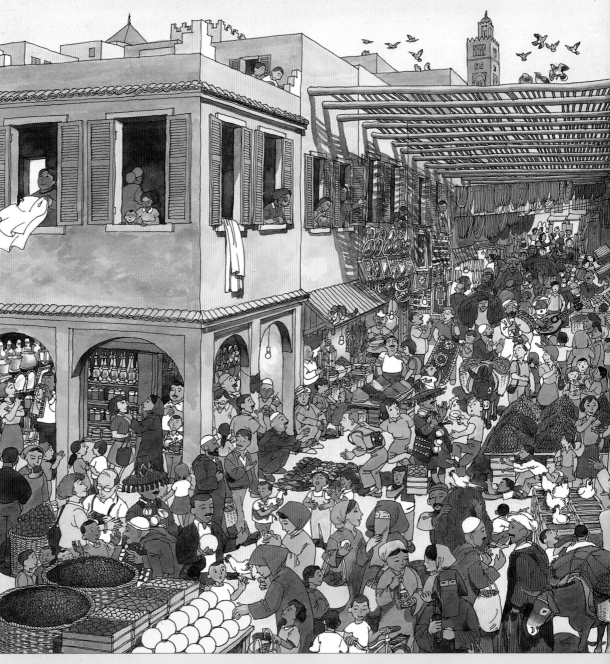

 Painted pottery

Woven baskets

Copper trays

Embroidered caps

Leather slippers called babouches

You can buy lovely handmade crafts and may even see some being made. Find where these things are being sold.

Horse riding has been popular here for hundreds of years. Spot two saddles for sale

20

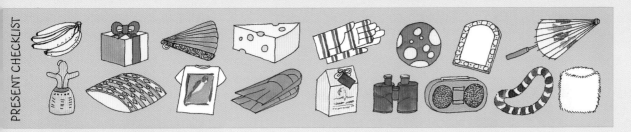

Water carriers go around selling cups of water to thirsty shoppers. Spot four.

Live animals are on sale. Find nine chickens.

People argue over the price of things. Spot two people bargaining for this carpet.

Can you spot where olives are being sold from huge baskets?

In the next place, you might sit out in the hot sun. Find a shady hat to wear.

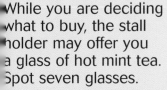

While you are deciding what to buy, the stall holder may offer you a glass of hot mint tea. Spot seven glasses.

Women buy powder for making up their eyes, lips and cheeks, and cedarwood containers to keep it in. Spot 12.

Cedarwood container

Bottles of powder

Great Aunt Marigold has bought lots of things. Can you find her?

At the mall

There are plenty of benches to sit on if you get tired. Spot eight.

At the information desk, people will help you find what you need. Can you see it?

The mall is so big, it's easy to get lost. Find a child who has lost his mother.

You can have your hair washed and cut at the hair salon. Can you spot it?

At this big, busy mall, you can do all your shopping without ever having to go outside. If you don't want to shop, you can eat or drink instead. Some people come to the mall to meet their friends and have a chat.

Kites

Books

Sports equipment

Jeans

Shoes

Cowboy hats

Flowers

Can you find where these things are for sale?

Cakes

Can you spot a group of cheerleaders putting on a show?

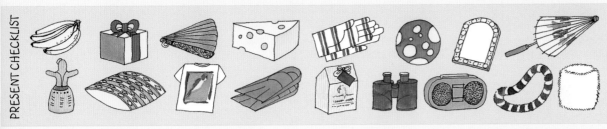

Paintings, called murals, make the walls look bright and interesting. Can you see one?

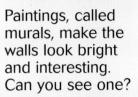

You can travel from one level to another in the glass elevator. Can you find it?

Spot five telephones.

Security guards check that there is no trouble in the mall. Spot ten.

In the next place, you might stay in a hotel. Find a new suitcase to put your things in.

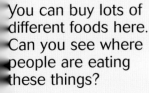

You can buy lots of different foods here. Can you see where people are eating these things?

Spaghetti

Ice cream

Pizza

Statues, plants and fountains make you feel as if you're outside. Spot 24 flamingo statues.

Going skiing

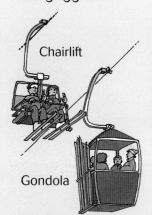

Snowmobiles are like little cars on skis. Spot five.

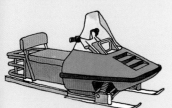

Goggles protect your eyes from the sun. Can you see someone who has broken his goggles?

Chairlift

Gondola

Chairlifts and gondolas take you to the top of steep slopes. Find four of each of these.

You can ride through the snow in a horse-drawn sleigh. Spot three.

Great Aunt Marigold isn't a very good skier. Can you see where she is?

This crowded ski resort is one of the liveliest places on your tour. You can have all kinds of fun skiing down the snowy slopes. There are lots of other sporty things to do too. But be careful that you don't bump into anyone.

There are kindergarten groups for children who are too young to ski. Spot two groups building snowmen.

Snowboarders use one wide board instead of two skis. Spot ten.

Snowboard

If you don't have your own skis, you can rent them. Find a ski-rental shop.

24

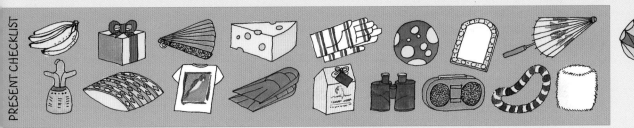

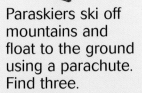

Paraskiers ski off mountains and float to the ground using a parachute. Find three.

Teachers called ski instructors give people skiing lessons. Spot two.

You can go sliding down the slopes on a toboggan. Find nine.

On gentle slopes, a drag lift pulls you up to the top. Spot three people on a drag lift.

In the next place, you'll be doing lots of shopping. Find this useful shopping bag.

Some people go climbing up the mountains. Spot three climbers with ice picks.

Ice pick

On frozen lakes, you can skate and play sports. Spot 30 people on skates.

There are hang-gliders in the sky. Spot three.

Great Aunt Marigold is about to take a photo. Can you see her?

On safari

When they spot a dead animal, vultures fly down to feed on it. Can you find 14?

Baboons live in groups called troops. They all look after the babies. Find 23.

Baobab trees store lots of water in their trunks. Spot two.

Cheetahs creep up on other animals before chasing them. Find five.

Agama lizards scuttle around in the grass or on rocks. Spot three.

Here, you're out in the open air, on the hot, dry, African plains. You've joined lots of other people on an exciting animal-watching trip called a safari. It's hard to believe there are so many amazing animals living in one place.

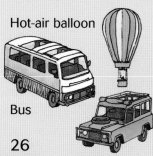

Hot-air balloon

Bus

On a safari, you can travel around in different ways. Spot three of each of these.

Truck

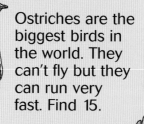

Ostriches are the biggest birds in the world. They can't fly but they can run very fast. Find 15.

Insects called termites build nests inside huge mounds of soil. Find four termite mounds

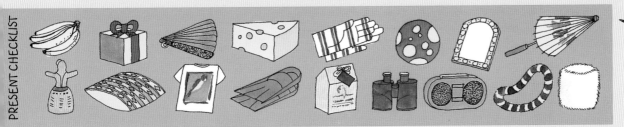

Weaverbirds make complicated nests out of lots of pieces of grass. Spot ten.

Lions like to lie in the shade. Can you find nine?

Zebra

Thomson's gazelle

Wildebeest

These animals eat grass nearly all day long. Spot 15 of each of them.

Scientists come here to find out about wildlife. Can you spot four?

You're going to an even drier place next. Find a bottle of water to take with you.

Wild dogs hunt together in groups called packs. Spot nine.

Elephants are so big, they need to eat a lot. Find 17.

Giraffes have to bend a long way down to reach water. Spot 13.

Great Aunt Marigold is busy making friends. Can you see her?

Town life

At the New Year, some people dress up and parade along the street. Find a dragon costume.

Pigs

Ducks

Can you see these animals being taken to market?

In China, there are steam trains, and newer diesel or electric trains too. Spot a steam train.

Many Chinese people are farmers. Spot ten farmers growing rice in paddy fields.

In this pretty town, there's a canal to walk along and some lovely gardens. As you wander around, you'll see people getting ready for the New Year Festival. They are shopping for presents and making decorations.

Tea grows in lots of parts of China and is a popular drink. Spot some teapots for sale.

Most people travel around the town on bicycles. Find 20.

Silk thread comes from caterpillars called silkworms. People weave it into soft cloth. Find some rolls of silk cloth.

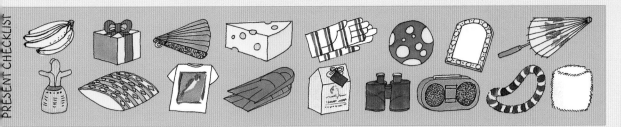

Giant pandas are very rare animals. Wild ones live only in China. Find a toy panda.

Some people keep birds. Find seven birdcages.

Find a group of people doing exercises called t'ai chi.

Many things are made out of bamboo. Can you find three of these bamboo baby buggies?

There will be lots of snow in the next place. Find a spade to clear a path.

A pagoda is a kind of tall tower. It's usually part of a temple. Can you see one?

Spot nine people carrying things in baskets hanging from a pole across their shoulders.

Find three kites.

Great Aunt Marigold is sitting in the shade. Find her.

Forest people

The Ashaninca travel up and down the river in canoes. They fish from them too. Find nine.

People paint their faces with red dye from the seeds of anatto plants. Spot a girl with an armful of anatto seeds.

Mothers often carry their babies in slings. Find nine babies in slings.

Many beautiful birds live in the forest. Some are kept as pets. Spot a girl with a pet parrot.

You've paddled up the River Amazon, right into the heart of the hot, sticky rainforest. The people living here are called the Ashaninca. They gather plants from the forest, hunt animals for food, and grow their own crops.

The main food is a plant called cassava, which is made into flour. Spot someone mashing up cassava with a pole.

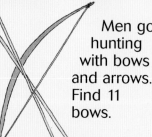

Men go hunting with bows and arrows. Find 11 bows.

The big thatched roofs are made from palm leaves. Can you see someone mending a roof?

PRESENT CHECKLIST

Families of red howler monkeys live in the forest. Spot 18 monkeys.

People sleep in hammocks. Can you find seven?

Wood is used to make houses, ladders, canoes, weapons and tools. Find someone chopping wood.

Children use catapults to shoot at birds. Find two.

Next, you're going to a big party. Find a feather garland to wear.

Houses are built on stilts above the ground, so people use ladders to climb up to them. Spot two ladders.

The Ashaninca grow cotton to make clothes, hammocks and slings. Find two people doing each of these things.

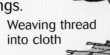

Spinning cotton into thread

Weaving thread into cloth

Island life

Great Aunt Marigold is busy exploring the island. Can you see where she is?

Donkeys are used for carrying things. Find eight.

Modern vases are often made to look like ancient Greek ones. Spot six big vases like this.

This musical instrument is a bouzouki. Can you find eight?

Yogurt and banana

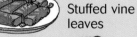

Stuffed vine leaves

Greek salad

Restaurants serve delicious food. Spot someone eating this meal.

Churches often have dome-shaped roofs. Find three.

This pretty island looks like an exciting place to stop for a while. You can explore the winding alleyways or climb up to the old castle on the hill. There are lots of people here. Some live on the island, and some are just visiting.

Women make lace and embroider cloths. They decorate their homes with these. Spot ten women sewing.

Leather bags

Can you see where these are being sold?

Necklaces

Postcards

Cats wander along streets and over rooftops. They like to sleep in the sun. Spot 12.

32

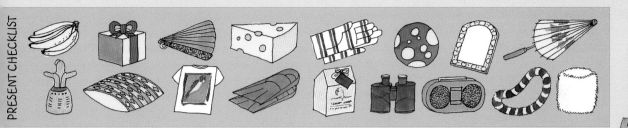

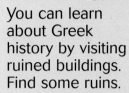

You can learn about Greek history by visiting ruined buildings. Find some ruins.

The only way to leave the island is by boat. Can you spot five little boats with oars?

Mediterranean monk seals are so rare, they are hardly ever seen. Can you find two?

When they are closed, shutters keep houses cool. Spot 11 windows with red shutters.

In the next place, you'll see lots of animals. Find a pad and crayons to draw them.

Many islanders make money from fishing. Find four of each of these things.

Fishing boats

Baskets of fish

Can you spot these people working?

Shoemaker

Baker

Tinsmith

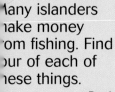

Great Aunt Marigold is stuck in traffic. Can you see her?

On the street

Monkeys, called langurs, scamper around the town, looking for food. Can you find 20?

Trains are often so crowded that people have to sit on top. Spot one.

Cycle rickshaw

Scooter rickshaw

Rickshaws are used as taxis. Spot eight of each of these types.

To say "hello", you put your hands together and bow your head. Spot 12 pairs of people saying hello.

You've arrived in the middle of the hustle and bustle of an Indian town. The streets are full of traffic and swarming with crowds. Plenty of rich people live here, but other people are so poor, they have to beg for money.

The old fort was built hundreds of years ago, to protect the town from enemies. Can you see it?

Tea is boiled in a pan with milk and sugar. Spices are often added. Spot the tea seller.

Can you spot 16 crows?

34

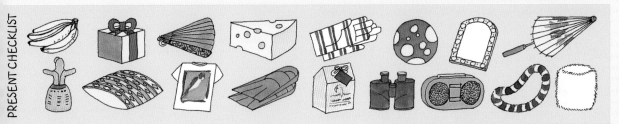

The cinema is very popular. Find this poster telling people what's on.

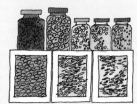

Can you see where these tasty sweetmeats are being sold?

Can you see where these tasty sweetmeats are being sold?

The street barber doesn't charge much to shave people. Find him.

A puri is a type of bread which is fried until it puffs up into a ball. Spot a man frying puris.

In the next place, the ground might be wet. Find a pair of deck shoes so you don't slip.

o worship, Hindus o to temples and Muslims go to osques. Find ne of each.

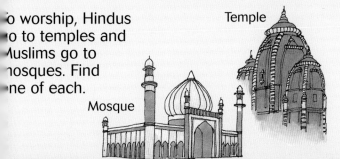

Temple

Mosque

Most Indians are Hindus. They believe that cows are holy, so let them wander wherever they want. Spot seven cows.

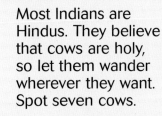

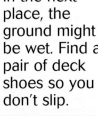

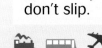

Dogs called laikas are used to pull sleds. Their thick coats keep them warm. Spot 32.

Balalaika

Accordion

Musicians entertain people at the races. Spot six of each of these musical instruments.

People fill oil drums with ice from the river. They melt it for water. Spot 20.

Siberia is very hard to get to. People often arrive here by helicopter. Can you spot two?

Great Aunt Marigold is admiring the reindeer. Can you see her?

Reindeer races

You've journeyed all the way north to Siberia. Everyone is celebrating the end of the long, cold winter with reindeer races on the frozen river. Many people here keep herds of reindeer. They make warm clothes from their skins.

Some herders follow their reindeer around as they look for food. They live in tents called chums. Find three.

Frozen rivers make good ice rinks. Can you spot 15 people skating?

There are huge forests in Siberia, so people make things out of wood. Spot three people chopping wood.

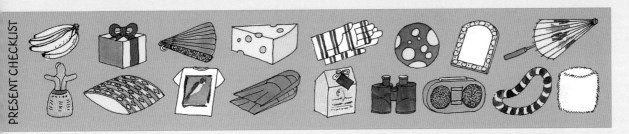

A samovar is a big metal pot for making tea. Can you see one?

Reindeer herders carve beautiful things from bone. Can you see someone carving?

Wild bears, wolves, elk and sable live in nearby forests. Find a toy bear.

Sliding along on skis is often easier than walking on snow. Spot ten people on skis.

The next place is cold and snowy too. Find some warm, furry earmuffs.

Trucks are good for driving on icy ground. Snowmobiles are used for shorter journeys. Find six of each.

Snowmobile

Truck

For the races, reindeer wear bright cloths and harnesses. Find someone dressing up his reindeer.

Cruising along

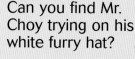

Can you find Mr. Choy trying on his white furry hat?

Muffin seems to like her yellow cushion. See if you can spot her.

Baby Nina is munching her bananas. Can you find her?

Great Aunt Eva loves her garland of flowers. Can you see where she is?

A painted parasol was just what Rosie wanted. Can you see her?

The last part of your journey is a trip on this luxury cruise ship. There are lots of things to do here. As a surprise, Great Aunt Marigold has invited all your friends and relations. Can you spot them with their presents?

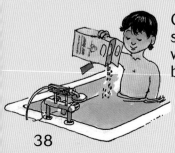

Can you spot Jack with his bath salts?

Jo is keeping cool with her fan. Find her.

Uncle Mike is looking out to sea through his blue binoculars. Can you find him?

Great Uncle Frank is already eating his chocolates. Can you see where he is?

Aunt Mimi is having fun with her flippers. Look hard and see if you can spot her.

Max is wearing his new T-shirt to play with some friends. Find him.

Spot Doctor Parekh chatting to someone about her clay statue.

Find the twins listening to their radio together.

Spot Sacha showing off his striped gloves.

Lennox is nibbling his cheese. Can you spot him?

Mrs. Choy is very pleased with her mirror. Can you see where she is?

Sniff is playing with his spotted ball. Find him.

Your tour is over! To say "thank you" to Great Aunt Marigold, you've bought her a new dress. Can you see her wearing it?

Great World Tour

Follow the numbers on the map to see the route you should have taken on your tour, and how you went from place to place.

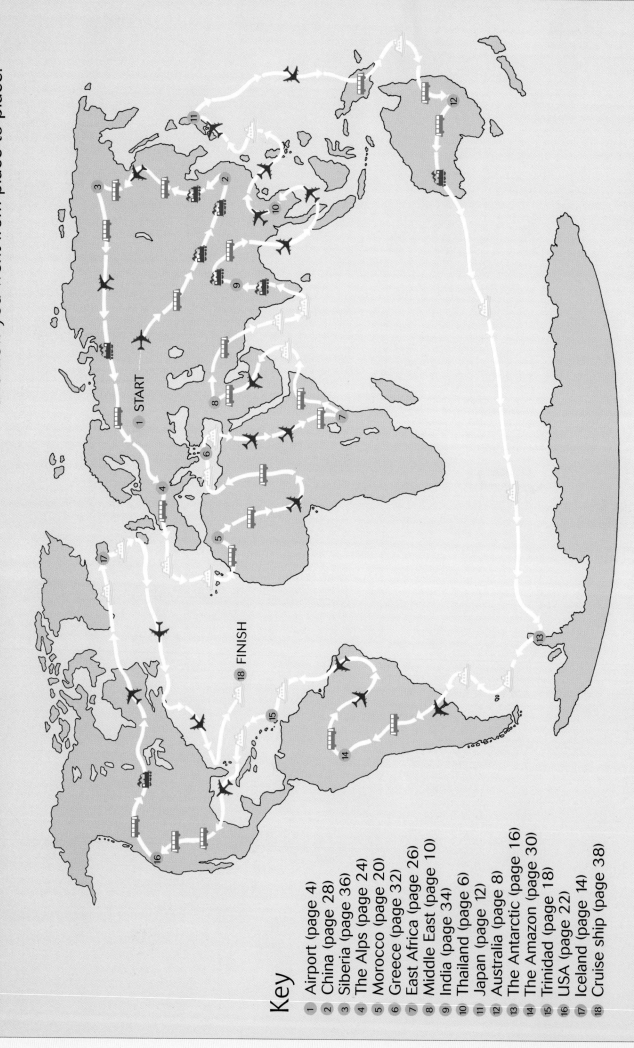

START

FINISH

Key

Extra puzzle

To do this puzzle, you'll need to look back through the book. Don't forget to look at the information strips on each double page. If you get stuck, you'll find the answers on page 48.

1. Which was the coldest place you visited?

2. Which was the hottest place you visited?

3. What was the earliest time you had to get up?

4. Which place were you in at 3:30pm?

5. How many snowy places did you visit?

6. How many sunny places did you visit?

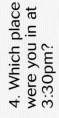

7. How many of each of these did you go on?

8. Which of these buildings is a hotel?

A   B   C   D   E   F

9. Which of these people saves other people's lives?

A   B   C   D   E   F   G

10. Which of these might be offered to you in the middle of a desert?

A   B   C   D   E   F

11. Which of these people is trying not to get sunburn?

A   B   C   D   E   F

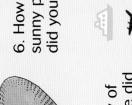

41

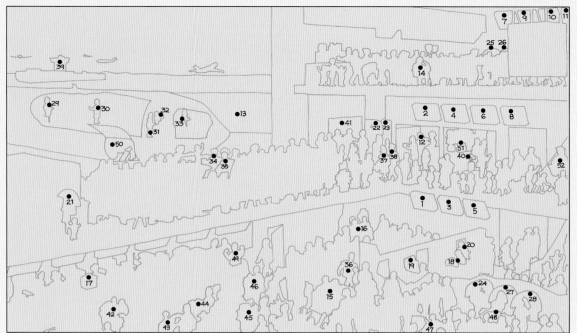

At the airport 4–5

Screens 1 2 3 4 5 6
7 8 9 10 11
Person buying
sunglasses 12
Covered walkway 13
Person eating meal
14
Buggies 15 16
Cat 17
Bag being searched
18
Knife on X-ray
machine 19
Person going
through metal
detector 20
Phones 21 22 23
24 25 26 27 28
Flight attendants 29
30 31 32 33 34
35 36 37 38
Control tower 39
Red flag 40
Bureau de change
41
Trolleys 42 43 44
45 46 47 48
Person with torn
ticket 49

Cargo hold 50
Big box of
chocolates 51
Great Aunt Marigold
52

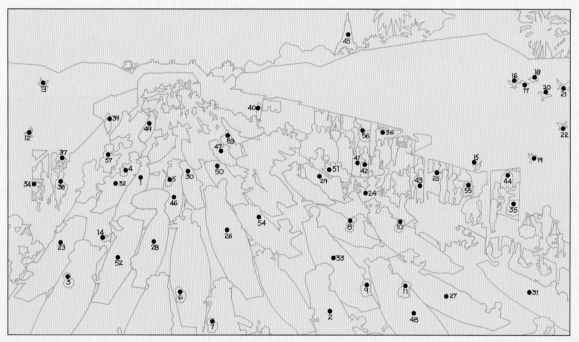

Floating market 6–7

Boats selling hats
1 2
Weighing scales 3 4
5 6 7 8 9 10 11
Purple-throated
sunbirds 12 13 14
15 16 17 18 19
20 21 22
Boats selling cooked
food 23 24
Corn on the cob
seller 25
Boats full of
watermelons 26 27
Boats full of
coconuts 28 29
Boats full of
pineapples 30 31
Boats full of limes
32 33
Wooden table 34
Embroidered
cushions 35
Silver necklaces 36
Lacquerware ducks
37
Buddhist monks 38
39 40 41 42 43
Silk jacket 44

Buddhist temple 45
Boats selling fish 46
47 48
Boats selling pots
and pans 49 50 51
Boats selling flowers
52 53 54
Dolls 55
Painted parasol 56
Great Aunt Marigold
57

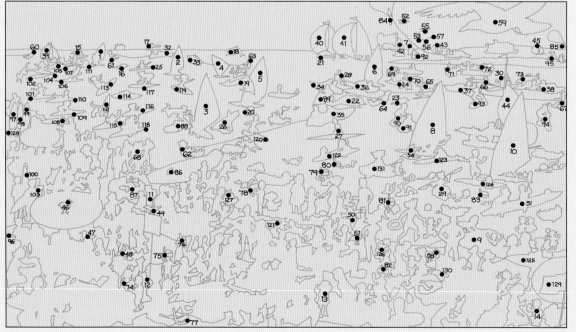

On the beach 8–9

Sailboards 1 2 3 4 5
6 7 8 9 10
People putting on
sunblock 11 12 13
14
Dolphins 15 16 17
18 19 20 21 22
23 24
Kayaks 25 26 27
28 29 30 31
Speedboats 32 33
34 35 36 37 38
Sailboats 39 40 41
42 43 44 45
Seagulls 46 47 48
49 50 51 52 53
54 55 56 57 58
59
Water-skiers 60 61
62 63 64 65 66
67
Lifesaver team 68
Divers 69 70 71 72
73
Snorkels 74 75 76
77 78 79 80 81
82 83
Parasailers 84 85
Camera 86

Jet skis 87 88 89 90
91 92 93 94 95
Surfboards 96 97
98 99 100 101
102 103 104 105
106 107 108 109
110 111 112 113
114 115 116 117
118 119 120 121
122 123 124 125
Toy koala 126
Toy kangaroo 127
Flags 128 129
Green flippers 130
Great Aunt Marigold
131

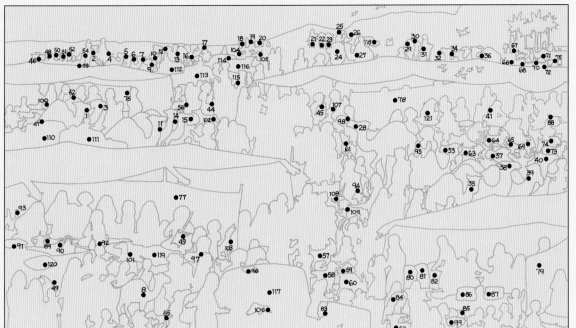

Desert homes 10–11

Camels 1 2 3 4 5 6
7 8 9 10 11 12 13
14 15 16 17 18 19
20 21 22 23 24
25 26 27 28 29
30 31 32 33 34
35 36 37 38 39
40
Person baking bread
41
Rababs 42 43 44
45
Goats 46 47 48 49
50 51 52 53 54
55 56 57 58 59
60 61 62 63 64
65 66 67 68 69
70 71 72 73 74
75
Sahahs 76 77 78 79
Sacks of dried food
80 81 82
Strings of onions 83
84 85
Metal cooking pots
86 87 88
Coffee pot 89
Ladle 90
Coffee cups 91

Pestle and mortar
92
Camel saddles 93
94 95
Book 96
Bowls of camel milk
97 98 99
Salukis 100 101
102 103 104 105
106 107 108 109
Trucks 110 111 112
113 114 115 116
117 118
Rug 119
Yellow cushion 120
Great Aunt Marigold
121

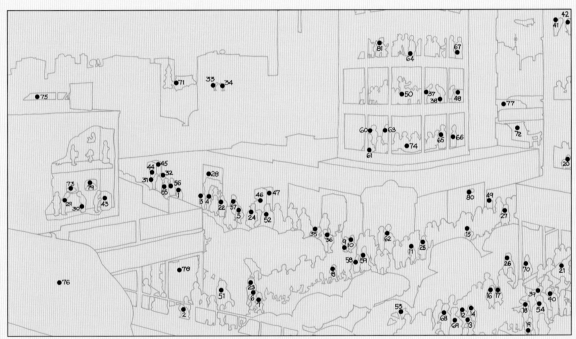

City lights 12–13

Schoolchildren 1 2
3 4 5 6 7 8 9 10
11 12 13 14 15 16
17 18 19 20
Sushi for sale 21
People wearing
masks 22 23 24 25
26 27
Chicken stall 28
People bowing 29
30 31 32 33 34
35 36 37 38 39
40 41 42
Vending machines
43 44 45 46 47
48 49
Karaoke bar 50
Sumo wrestlers 51
52 53 54
Kimonos 55 56 57
58 59 60 61 62
63 64 65 66 67
68 69 70
Temple 71
Shrine 72
Towel 73
Traditional restaurant
74

Bullet trains 75 76
77
Place selling
computers 78
Person asleep 79
Radio 80
Great Aunt Marigold
81

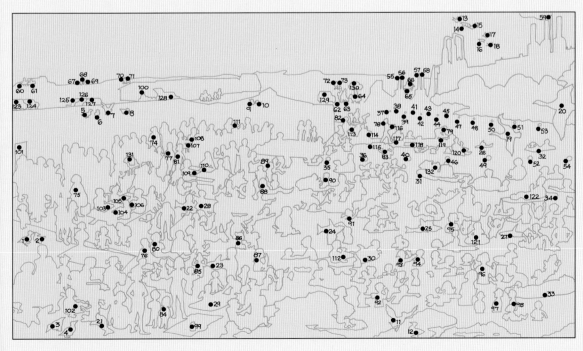

At the pool 14–15

Eider ducks 1 2 3 4
5 6 7 8 9 10 11
12 13 14 15 16 17
18 19 20
Toy sharks 21 22
23 24 25 26 27
Inflatable beds 28
29 30 31 32 33
34
Buoys 35 36 37 38
39 40 41 42 43
44 45 46 47 48
49 50 51 52 53
54
Pipes blowing out
steam 55 56 57 58
59
People horse riding
60 61 62 63 64
65 66
People hiking 67 68
69 70 71 72 73
Doctor 74
Person who has
bought face cream
75
Waiters 76 77 78
79

Waitresses 80 81
82 83
People with mud on
their faces 84 85
86 87 88 89 90
91 92 93 94 95
96 97 98
Sea-sickness pills 99
Man arriving at hotel
100
Women's changing
rooms 101
Food trays 102 103
104 105 106 107
108 109 110 111
112 113 114 115
116 117 118 119
120 121 122
Trucks 123 124 125
126 127 128 129
130
Bath salts 131
Great Aunt Marigold
132

43

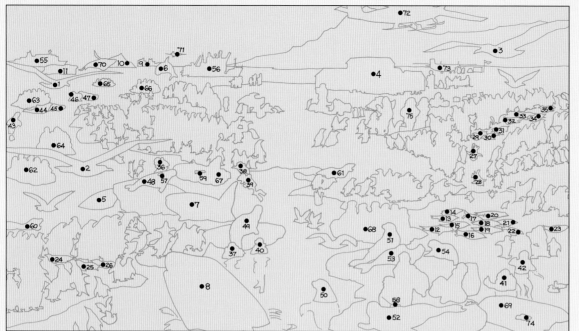

Frozen land 16–17

Albatrosses 1 2 3
Research station 4
Killer whales 5 6 7
8
Castle iceberg 9
Pyramid iceberg 10
Greek temple
iceberg 11
Penguins porpoising
12 13 14 15 16 17
18 19 20 21 22
23
Penguins
tobogganing 24 25
26 27 28 29 30
31 32 33 34 35
Divers 36 37 38 39
40 41 42
Crabeater seals 43
44 45 46 47 48
49 50 51 52 53
54
Cruise ship 55
Research ship 56
Satellite tags 57 58
Flashlight 59
Leopard seals 60 61
Dinghies 62 63 64
65 66 67 68 69

Humpback whale 70
Planes 71 72 73
Striped gloves 74
Great Aunt Marigold
75

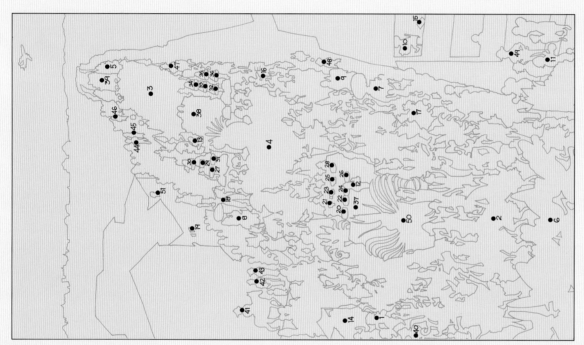

Carnival! 18–19

Great Aunt Marigold
1
Underwater group 2
Circus group 3
Incas group 4
Spanish dancing
group 5
Flying animals group
6
Fruit sorbet 7
Corn on the cob 8
Roti 9
Person pretending to
be a judge 10
Coconut seller 11
People singing 12 13
Fruit stall 14
Calculator 15
Jab Molassi 16
Burroquite 17
Moco Jumbie 18
Pans 19 20 21 22
23 24 25 26 27
28 29 30 31 32
33 34 35 36
Floats 37 38 39
Policemen 40 41 42
43 44 45 46 47
48 49

Amazing costume
50
T-shirt 51

Shady souk 20–21

Herbs and spices 1
Lute 2
Drum 3
People carrying wool
4 5 6
Dates for sale 7
Copper trays 8
Painted pottery 9
Leather slippers 10
Woven baskets 11
Embroidered caps 12
Saddles 13 14
Glasses of mint tea
15 16 17 18 19
20 21
Cedarwood
containers 22 23
24 25 26 27 28
29 30 31 32 33
Shady hat 34
Olives 35
People bargaining
36 37
Chickens 38 39 40
41 42 43 44 45
46
Water carriers 47
48 49 50
Mirror 51

Great Aunt Marigold
52

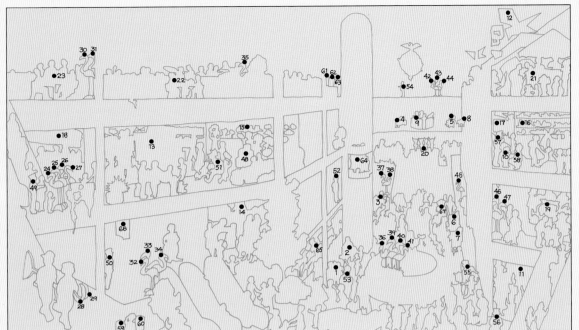

At the mall 22–23

Benches 1 2 3 4 5
6 7 8
Information desk 9
Lost child 10
Hair salon 11
Kites 12
Sports equipment 13
Books 14
Cowboy hats 15
Shoes 16
Jeans 17
Flowers 18
Cakes 19
Group of
cheerleaders 20
Ice cream 21
Spaghetti 22
Pizza 23
Flamingo statues 24
25 26 27 28 29
30 31 32 33 34
35 36 37 38 39
40 41 42 43 44
45 46 47
Suitcase 48
Security guards 49
50 51 52 53 54
55 56 57 58

Telephones 59 60
61 62 63
Glass elevator 64
Mural 65
Spotted ball 66
Great Aunt Marigold
67

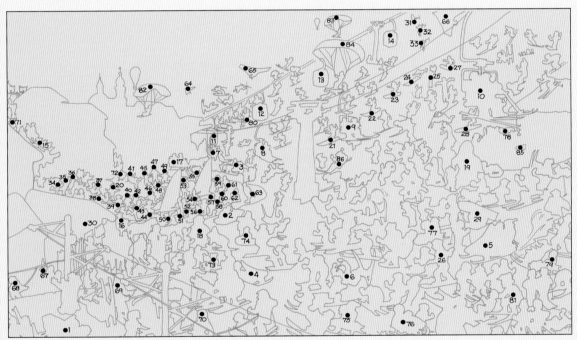

Going skiing 24–25

Snowmobiles 1 2 3
4 5
Broken goggles 6
Chairlifts 7 8 9 10
Gondolas 11 12 13
14
Sleighs 15 16 17
Groups building
snowmen 18 19
Snowboarders 20
21 22 23 24 25
26 27 28 29
Ski-rental shop 30
Climbers 31 32 33
People on skates 34
35 36 37 38 39
40 41 42 43 44
45 46 47 48 49
50 51 52 53 54
55 56 57 58 59
60 61 62 63
Hang-gliders 64 65
66
Shopping bag 67
People on drag lift
68 69 70
Toboggans 71 72
73 74 75 76 77
78 79

Ski instructors 80
81
Paraskiers 82 83 84
Cheese 85
Great Aunt Marigold
86

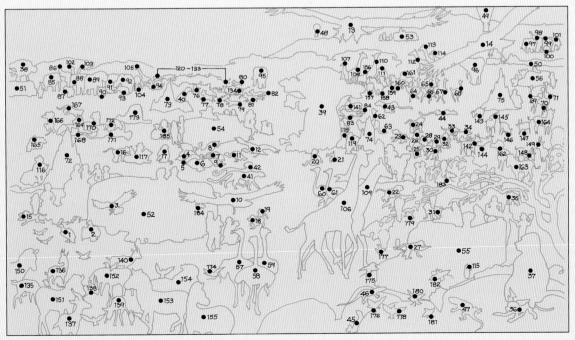

On safari 26–27

Vultures 1 2 3 4 5 6 7
8 9 10 11 12 13 14
Baboons 15 16 17 18
19 20 21 22 23 24
25 26 27 28 29 30
31 32 33 34 35 36
37
Baobab trees 38 39
Cheetahs 40 41 42 43
44
Agama lizards 45 46
47
Hot-air balloons 48 49
50
Buses 51 52 53
Trucks 54 55 56
Ostriches 57 58 59 60
61 62 63 64 65 66
67 68 69 70 71
Termite mounds 72 73
74 75
Wild dogs 76 77 78
79 80 81 82 83 84
Elephants 85 86 87
88 89 90 91 92 93
94 95 96 97 98 99
100 101
Giraffes 102 103 104
105 106 107 108
109 110 111 112 113
114

Water bottle 115
Scientists 116 117 118
119
Wildebeest 120 121
122 123 124 125
126 127 128 129 130
131 132 133 134
Thomson's gazelles
135 136 137 138 139
140 141 142 143 144
145 146 147 148 149
Zebras 150 151 152
153 154 155 156 157
158 159 160 161
162 163 164
Lions 165 166 167
168 169 170 171
172 173
Weaverbirds 174 175
176 177 178 179 180
181 182 183
Blue binoculars 184
Great Aunt Marigold
185

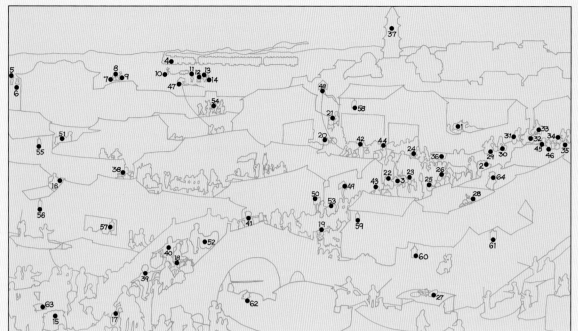

Town life 28–29

Dragon costume 1
Pigs 2
Ducks 3
Steam train 4
Farmers 5 6 7 8 9
   10 11 12 13 14
Teapots for sale 15
Bicycles 16 17 18
   19 20 21 22 23
   24 25 26 27 28
   29 30 31 32 33
   34 35
Rolls of silk cloth 36
Pagoda 37
People with baskets
on poles 38 39 40
   41 42 43 44 45
   46
Kites 47 48 49
Spade 50
Baby buggies 51 52
   53
T'ai chi group 54
Birdcages 55 56 57
   58 59 60 61
Toy panda 62
Wooden fan 63
Great Aunt Marigold
   64

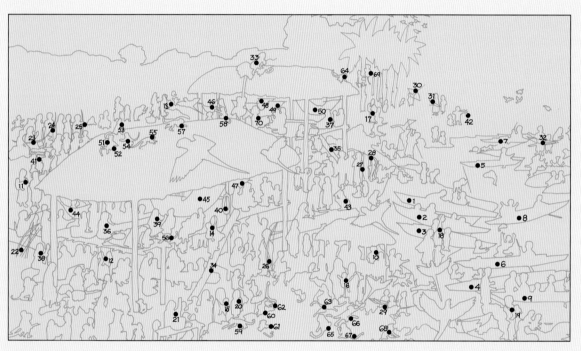

Forest people 30–31

Canoes 1 2 3 4 5 6
   7 8 9
Girl with anatto
seeds 10
Babies in slings 11
   12 13 14 15 16 17
   18 19
Girl with parrot 20
Person mashing up
cassava 21
Bows 22 23 24 25
   26 27 28 29 30
   31 32
Person mending roof
   33
Ladders 34 35
People weaving 36
   37
People spinning 38
   39
Feather garland 40
Catapults 41 42
Person chopping
wood 43
Hammocks 44 45
   46 47 48 49 50

Red howler monkeys
   51 52 53 54 55
   56 57 58 59 60
   61 62 63 64 65
   66 67 68
Bunch of bananas
   69
Great Aunt Marigold
   70

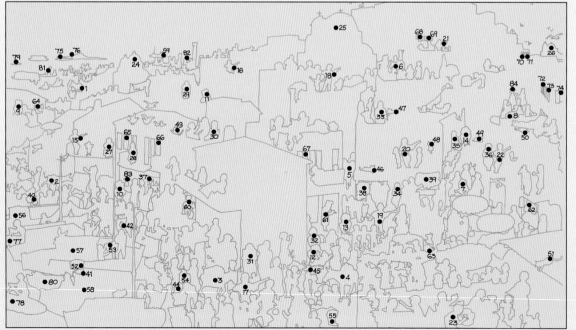

Island life 32–33

Donkeys 1 2 3 4 5
   6 7 8
Vases 9 10 11 12 13
   14
Bouzoukis 15 16 17
   18 19 20 21 22
Person eating meal
   23
Churches 24 25 26
Women sewing 27
   28 29 30 31 32
   33 34 35 36
Necklaces 37
Postcards 38
Leather bags 39
Cats 40 41 42 43
   44 45 46 47 48
   49 50 51
Baskets of fish 52
   53 54 55
Fishing boats 56 57
   58 59
Tinsmith 60
Baker 61
Shoemaker 62
Pad and crayons 63

Windows with red
shutters 64 65 66
   67 68 69 70 71
   72 73 74
Mediterranean monk
seals 75 76
Boats with oars 77
   78 79 80 81
Ruins 82
Clay statue 83
Great Aunt Marigold
   84

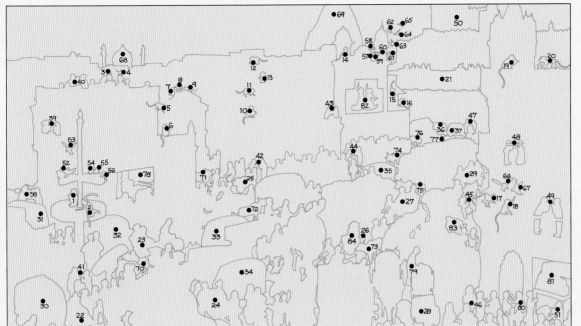

On the street 34–35

Langurs 1 2 3 4 5 6
7 8 9 10 11 12 13
14 15 16 17 18 19
20
Train 21
Cycle rickshaws 22
23 24 25 26 27
28 29
Scooter rickshaws
30 31 32 33 34
35 36 37
Pairs of people
saying hello 38 39
40 41 42 43 44
45 46 47 48 49
Old fort 50
Tea seller 51
Crows 52 53 54 55
56 57 58 59 60
61 62 63 64 65
66 67
Mosque 68
Temple 69
Cows 70 71 72 73
74 75 76 77
Deck shoes 78
Man frying puris 79
Street barber 80
Sweetmeats 81

Cinema poster 82
Garland of flowers
83
Great Aunt Marigold
84

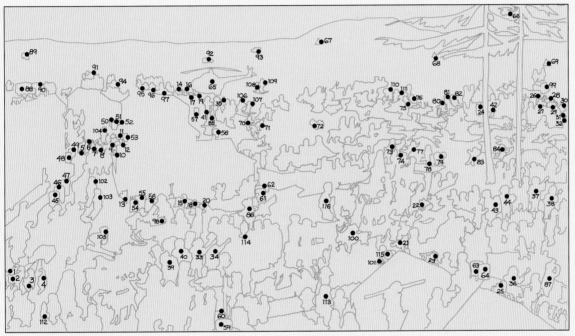

Reindeer races 36–37

Laikas 1 2 3 4 5 6
7 8 9 10 11 12 13
14 15 16 17 18 19
20 21 22 23 24
25 26 27 28 29
30 31 32
Balalaikas 33 34 35
36 37 38
Accordions 39 40
41 42 43 44
Oil drums 45 46 47
48 49 50 51 52
53 54 55 56 57
58 59 60 61 62
63 64
Helicopters 65 66
Chums 67 68 69
People skating 70
71 72 73 74 75
76 77 78 79 80
81 82 83 84
People chopping
wood 85 86 87
Trucks 88 89 90 91
92 93
Snowmobiles 94 95
96 97 98 99
Person dressing up
reindeer 100

Earmuffs 101
People on skis 102
103 104 105
106 107 108 109
110 111
Toy bear 112
Person carving 113
Samovar 114
White furry hat 115
Great Aunt Marigold
116

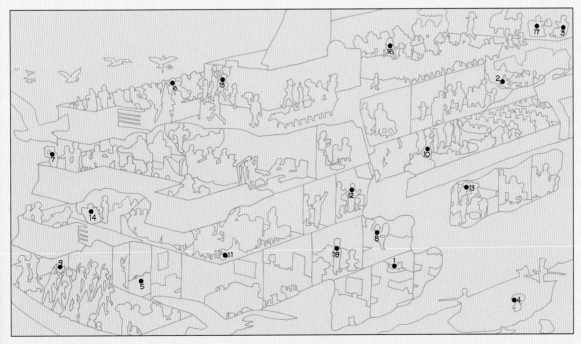

Cruising along 38–39

Muffin 1
Baby Nina 2
Great Aunt Eva 3
Rosie 4
Jack 5
Jo 6
Uncle Mike 7
Mrs. Choy 8
Sniff 9
Great Aunt Marigold
10
Lennox 11
Sacha 12
The twins 13
Doctor Parekh 14
Max 15
Aunt Mimi 16
Great Uncle Frank 17
Mr. Choy 18

Acknowledgements

The publishers would like to thank the following organizations and individuals for their help in the preparation of this book:

pages 4–5: Roz Quade, BAA London Gatwick, England

pages 8–9: Australian Tourist Commission, London, England

pages 10–11: Shelagh Weir, Curator for the Middle East, Museum of Mankind (British Museum), London, England

pages 12–13: Ms Mitsuko Ohno

pages 14–15: Blue Lagoon Ltd, PO Box 22, 240 Grindavik, Iceland

pages 16–17: Sheila Anderson

pages 18–19: Trinidad High Commissioner's Office, London, England

pages 20–21: The Best of Morocco

pages 24–25: David Hearns, Ski Club of Great Britain, London, England

pages 26–27: David Duthie

pages 28–29: Frances Wood, Curator of the Chinese Collections, British Library, London, England

pages 30–31: Survival, 6 Charterhouse Buildings, London EC1N 7ET, England, UK. For more information about Rainforest people, visit www.survival-international.org

pages 32–33: Andrew Stoddart, The Hellenic Bookservice, 91 Fortress Road, London NW5 1AG, England

pages 34–35: A.K. Singh, Indian Tourist Board, London, England

pages 36–37: Dr Alan Wood, University of Lancaster, England

pages 38–39: Tim Stocker, P&O Cruises, 77 New Oxford Street, London WC1A 1PP, England

Answers to Extra puzzle on page 41

1. Siberia

2. East Africa

3. 8 a.m. (Thailand)

4. Airport

5. Three (The Antarctic, The Alps, Siberia)

6. Five (Middle East, Trinidad, Morocco, East Africa, Greece)

7. 18 boats; 20 planes; 8 trains; 22 buses

8. D

9. F

10. C

11. F

Cover and additional design by Stephanie Jones • Additional editing by Ben Denne • Proofreading by Claire Masset